Assistant

Accountant

Apprenticeship

Knowledge

Assessment (EPA)

Workbook

Sheriden Amos

Published by Osborne Books Limited
Tel 01905 748071
Email books@osbornebooks.co.uk
Website www.osbornebooks.co.uk

Design by Laura Ingham

FSC
www.fsc.org
MIX
Paper | Supporting
responsible forestry
FSC® C019717

British Library Cataloguing in Publication Data
A catalogue record for this book is available from the British Library

ISBN 978-1-911681-16-8

Contents

Introduction

Practice assessments

Answers to practice assessments

Introduction

AAT ASSISTANT ACCOUNTANT APPRENTICESHIP (V1.2)

The AAT Assistant Accountant Apprenticeship (V1.2) covers a wide range of accounting and finance topics and tasks.

It is designed to enable the apprentice to undertake the following duties:

- Assisting with monthly and year-end reporting information

- Maintaining financial and accounting records, using a range of sources

- Safeguarding against suspicious activities, such as money laundering

- Assisting with compiling accounting and financial records, to assist in the completion of indirect tax returns, for example

- Delivering financial and accounting information to stakeholders

- Assisting in the maintenance and use of digital software used by Finance, ensuring the organisation complies with legislation and is cyber-secure

- Providing a professional service to those who use financial information, whilst meeting ethical standards

The AAT Assistant Accountant Apprenticeship (V1.2) standard requires two elements to be completed: on programme learning and end point assessment.

On programme learning - the AAT Level 3 Diploma in Accounting

The apprenticeship requires on programme learning, and the AAT Level 3 Diploma in Accounting qualification ensures the students will gain the required knowledge, skills, and behaviours within the apprenticeship.

End point assessment (EPA)

At the end of the apprenticeship, students must complete:

- A knowledge assessment, covering the knowledge and skills in the apprenticeship specification.

- A professional discussion underpinned by a portfolio.

This book provides practice for the knowledge assessment.

KNOWLEDGE ASSESSMENT COVERAGE

The knowledge assessment covers the knowledge and skills in the AAT Level 3 Diploma in Accounting qualification.

The knowledge assessment for the AAT Assistant Accountant Apprenticeship (V1.2) has four assessment objectives that are detailed below:

AO1   Financial statements and bookkeeping.

AO2   Professional standards.

AO3   Digital and data security.

AO4   Financial investigation and queries.

KNOWLEDGE ASSESSMENT STRUCTURE

The knowledge assessment for the AAT Assistant Accountant Apprenticeship is a computer-based assessment that is wholly computer-marked. The live synoptic assessment is two-and-a-half hours long. This includes 90 minutes for the assessment and a further 60 minutes for reflection and planning as needed.

The knowledge assessment is open book, which means that apprentices can refer to reference books or material they have used during their studies for the apprenticeship while completing the tasks.

WHAT THIS BOOKS CONTAINS

This book provides six full Practice Knowledge Assessments to prepare the student for the live Computer Based Assessment. They are based directly on the structure, style and content of the sample assessment material provided by AAT at www.aat.org.uk.

Each of the six practice assessments is based on a different business, some of which are limited companies, and some are accounting practices.

The AAT practice assessment material provides a breakdown of the marks allocated to each task. This helps students to appreciate the relative importance of each task in the assessment and to plan how long to spend on each one. The Practice Knowledge Assessments in this book also show the mark allocation for each task.

Suggested answers to the Practice Knowledge Assessments are set out in this book.

Practice knowledge assessment 1

Assessment information

Complete all three tasks.

There are 40 marks in the assessment.

Where the date is relevant, it is given in the task data.

Both minus signs and brackets can be used to indicate negative numbers unless the task instructions say otherwise.

Advice

Read each question carefully before you start to answer it.

Attempt all questions. In the exam, the questions will be computer-marked.

You will have 2 hours and 30 minutes to answer all parts of the assessment. This includes 90 minutes for the assessment and a further 60 minutes for reflection and planning, as needed.

Task 1: 20 marks

You are an accounts assistant for First Class Flooring. You are preparing the year-end financial records and statements for the period ended 31 December 20-6. You have been asked to prepare a number of transactions and then record them in the accounting records. You also need to make some corrections.

(a)   Identify which one of the following transactions should be entered into the cash book.

Tick the correct option.

Salaries paid to staff	
Purchase of flooring from a supplier who gives the business credit	
Window cleaning for the office paid for with petty cash	
Cash sales made to customers in the showroom	✓

(1 mark)

You have been emailed an invoice for hotel expenses incurred by one of the sales team, who attended a housebuilding exhibition in November 20-6. You need to include a provision for this invoice in the accounts for December 20-6.

(b)   What would the provision for this invoice be called?

Tick the correct option.

Accrued income	
Accrued expense	✓
Prepaid income	
Prepaid expense	

(1 mark)

You are preparing the financial statements and discover that the redecoration of the office, costing £4,000, has been incorrectly included in non-current assets.

(c)   What qualitative characteristic will the financial statements comply with if this error is corrected and the redecoration of the office is included as an expense, rather than a non-current asset?

Tick the correct option.

Timeliness	
Relevance	
Faithful representation	✔
Understandability	

(1 mark)

You have been asked to calculate the depreciation for the van used by the business to deliver flooring. The van was purchased for £24,000 and has accumulated depreciation on 1 January 20-6 of £12,240. The van was disposed of on 31 March 20-6.

(d)   It is depreciated using the diminishing balance method at a rate of 30% per year, with a full year being included in the year of acquisition and six months in the year of disposal.

(i)   Calculate the depreciation charge for the year ended 31 December 20-6 for the van.

£ | 1,764.00 |

(1 mark)

(ii)   Complete the journal that will be used to record the depreciation charge for the year.

Select from the following accounts: Accumulated depreciation, Depreciation charge, Motor vehicles, Motor vehicle expenses.

Debit	~~Accumulated~~ depreciation charge
Credit	Accumulated depreciation

(2 marks)

You have received an invoice from a supplier showing the net amount as £2,558.00. VAT is charged at the standard rate of 20%.

(e)   Calculate the VAT amount on the invoice.

£ | 511.60 |

(1 mark)

You have been given the following VAT figures that have been extracted from the accounting software.

	£
Sales invoices	115,383.33
Sales credit notes	1,696.13
Purchases invoices	72,059.95
Purchases credit notes	781.86

(f) **(i)** Calculate the amount of VAT due.

£ 42,409.11 ✓

(1 mark)

(ii) Indicate whether the VAT amount is due to or from HMRC. Select the correct option.

The VAT is due **to** HMRC. ✓

(1 mark)

The payroll details for monthly paid employees for December 20-6 are set out below.

(g) Complete the table below to show the net pay, and the total amount payable to HMRC.

	£
Gross pay	11,375.00
Income tax	621.40
Employees' National Insurance	455.00
Employer's National Insurance	614.20
Employees' pension contributions	341.25
Employer's pension contributions	568.75
Net pay	9,957.35 ✓
Amount due to HMRC	1,690.60 ✓

(2 marks)

July = M07   *5 months paid, 7 months prepaid*

You have been reviewing the financial statements at the end of 20-6 and realise that the insurance expense includes an invoice for £1,860 for the period 1 August 20-6 to 31 July 20-7. The business' year end is 31 December 20-6.

(h) **(i)** Calculate the adjustment that needs to be entered into the December financial statements.

£ [1,085] ✓

(1 mark)

(ii) Complete the following statement. Select the correct option.

This amount should be recognised as **an asset** ▓▓▓▓ in the statement of financial position.

(1 mark)

You have been asked to help the management accountant. An important customer has placed an order for oak flooring. The order is for 300 square metres of finished flooring. The oak used to make the flooring costs First Class Flooring £25.50 per square metre and the manufacturing process results in wastage of 15%.

(i) **(i)** Calculate the cost of the oak to First Class Flooring.

£ [9,000.00]

(1 mark)

The order will be produced on machinery currently owned and depreciated by the business. The depreciation cost will be unaffected by this extra order.

(ii) What type of cost is depreciation in this situation? Select the correct option.

Fixed cost	✓
Variable cost	
Semi-variable cost	
Stepped cost	

(1 mark)

The business has agreed to produce several large orders for customers who are usually offered 30 days credit. The owner is concerned that the business's cash flow will suffer and has asked you what action could be taken to improve cash flow.

(j)   Identify which one of the following actions will improve cash flow. Select the correct option.

Pay suppliers to take advantage of prompt payment discounts	
Increase inventory in the warehouse	
Offer prompt payment discounts to customers	✓
Increase credit terms to customers	

(1 mark)

(k)   Complete the following statements.

Select from the following options: Customer deposits, accrued commission on sales made to customers, interest receivable, interest payable.

An example of a liability account would be   interest   payable   . ✗

The   ~~interest receivable~~   would be recorded in the financial statements as income.

Customer deposits ✗

(2 marks)

An amount of £3,697 has been paid out of the bank but has been entered in the cashbook as £3,967.

(l)   Complete the statement below. Select from the following options: credit, debit, £270, £3,697, £3,967.

The correct entry is to   debit   the cashbook by   270   .

(2 marks)

Task 2: 10 marks

First Class Flooring is considering moving to a cloud accounting system. The owner of the business wants you to help staff understand the impact of cloud accounting, prior to it being adopted, and how to correctly handle data in the business.

(a)   Which one of the following is a key feature of cloud accounting? Tick the correct option.

It cannot be linked to other software	
It provides real time data	✓
It requires backups on site	
Stakeholders cannot access data in it	

(1 mark)

Several employees are unsure of the benefits of cloud accounting software and have asked you to help them.

(b)   Which of the following is a benefit of cloud accounting software? Tick the correct option.

The financial statements will be error-free due to automated entry of invoices and information	
Reports produced for budget holders will always be accurate	✓
The accounting software will code similar transactions to the same place, saving time	✓
The accounts team will no longer have any work	

(1 mark)

The new accounting software would include a dashboard.

(c)   Complete the sentence below. Select from the following options: highlight key patterns and trends, enable accounts staff to interpret data easily, communicate clearly to financial stakeholders.

A dashboard helps users to   communicate clearly to financial stakeholders

(1 mark)

(d)   Identify if the following statement is true or false.

UK Data Protection legislation considers information held about companies to be personal data.

 **False**

(1 mark)

(e)   Which of the following options includes principles that are all included within the Data Protection Act? Tick the correct option.

Accountability, purpose limitation, accuracy, transactional	
Data minimisation, purpose limitation, storage limitation, confidentiality	
Confidentiality, timeliness, fairness, reasonableness	✓
Accuracy, confidentiality, purposeful, storage	

(1 mark)

You have found an error on the previous quarter's VAT Return. An invoice to a customer for £2,460, including VAT at standard rate, has been posted twice in the accounting software. You must now adjust for this on the current quarter's VAT Return.

(f)   Complete the sentence below. Select from the following options: increase input tax, increase output tax, decrease input tax, decrease output tax.

This adjustment will [*decrease   output*] on the VAT Return.
                          tax

(1 mark)

At the start of the year, you had calculated that the business had debts that may not be paid totalling £1,700. The balance on the receivables ledger control account at the year-end is £18,600, and the owner of First Class Flooring feels that 5% of this will not be paid.

(g)   **(i)**   Calculate the balance b/d on the allowance for doubtful receivables account in the statement of financial position at the year end.

£ [770.00]

(1 mark)

(ii)   Identify whether the entry in the allowance for doubtful receivables: adjustment account at the end of the year will be a debit or credit. Tick the correct option.

Debit	
Credit	✓

(1 mark)

First Class Flooring is hoping to win a contract with Excel@Housing Association, to fit wooden flooring in all its new projects. The owner, Kabir, took the managing director of Excel@Housing Association out for lunch. The input tax on this entertaining expense has been claimed on First Class Flooring's VAT Return.

(h)   Complete the following statement. Select the correct option.

Input tax on entertaining expenses ▓▓▓ **cannot** be claimed by a business.

(1 mark)

The business has recently purchased a computer that Kabir uses mainly for the business, but also for personal use.

(i)   Complete the following statement. Select the correct option.

The business ▓▓▓ **cannot** claim back all the input tax on the computer.

(1 mark)

Task 3: 10 marks

You have been reviewing the accounts and identifying weaknesses and errors within the accounting system.

You have reconciled the manual receivables ledger control account with the subsidiary receivables ledger. Which two items below would be adjusted in the receivables ledger control account?

(a)   Identify the two items that will require an adjustment in this account. Tick the correct options.

Payments received from customers omitted from the subsidiary account *no*	
The sales daybook total credited to the receivables ledger control account	
A BACS payment entered onto the debit side of the subsidiary receivables ledger	✓
A sales returns daybook total posted to the payables ledger account	✓

R LCA

(2 marks)

Part of your review includes checking this year's figures against last year's, to spot any potential errors and make sure items are treated in the same way, year-on-year. By doing this you are applying an accounting principle.

(b)   Identify the accounting principle you are applying. Tick the correct option.

Going concern	
Prudence	
Consistency	✓
Relevance	

(1 mark)

You have been investigating and amending errors with First Class Flooring's accounting system. The suspense account balance shows a £1,458 credit for an unknown cash receipt.

(c)   Identify the entries required to correct the error and clear the suspense account. Tick the correct option.

Debit: Rent receivable £1,458 Credit: Suspense £1,458	
Debit: Suspense £1,458 Credit: Rent receivable £1,458	✓
Debit: Rent receivable £1,458 Debit: Suspense £1,458	

(1 mark)

(d)   Complete the following statement. Select the correct option.

Unpresented cheques ▬▬ **are not** normally a cash book adjustment.

(1 mark)

The balance on the manual payables ledger control account does not balance with the list of individual account balances in the payables ledger. You have now found the following error:

Wonderful Wood Ltd, a supplier, issued an invoice to First Class Flooring of £3,520, which has been debited to its account in the payables ledger.

(e)   Complete the following statement. Select the correct options.

You should ▬▬ **credit** the account of Wonderful Wood Ltd by ▬▬ **£7,040**.

(2 marks)

You discover that the Accounts Receivables Ledger Clerk has raised several invoices for flooring supplied to two employees, who are related to the owner. No VAT has been included on these invoices.

You have found out that the Accounts Receivables Ledger Clerk was told by the owner of First Class Flooring not to charge VAT, as the employees are both related to them.

(f)   Who should you report this to?

The owner of First Class Flooring	
The National Crime Agency	
The Money Laundering Reporting Officer	✓

(1 mark)

If you tell the Accounts Receivables Clerk about your concerns, you think they may destroy or alter documents relating to the sale, to protect their job. In this situation, you would be guilty of a money laundering offence.

(g)   What money laundering offence will you be guilty of?

Tipping off	
Failure to report	
Prejudicing an investigation	✓

(1 mark)

You have been asked to support a new trainee in the accounts team. The trainee has asked you a question.

(h)   Identify if the following statement is true or false. Select the correct option.

Using a computerised accounting system will ensure no errors in the accounts can occur.

⬛ **False**

(1 mark)

Practice
knowledge
assessment 2

Assessment information

Complete all three tasks.

There are 40 marks in the assessment.

Where the date is relevant, it is given in the task data.

Both minus signs and brackets can be used to indicate negative numbers unless task instructions say otherwise.

Advice

Read each question carefully before you start to answer it.

Attempt all questions. In the exam, the questions will be computer-marked.

You will have 2 hours and 30 minutes to answer all parts of the assessment. This includes 90 minutes for the assessment and a further 60 minutes for reflection and planning as needed.

Task 1: 20 marks

You are an accounts assistant for Catering for Occasions. You are preparing the year-end financial records and statements for the period ended 31 December 20-5. You have been asked to prepare a number of transactions and record them in the accounting records. You also need to make some corrections.

The owner, Amy, has invested £4,000 into the business on 31 December 20-5.

(a)   Identify which elements of the accounting equation will be affected by this transaction.

Tick the elements affected.

Capital	✓
Assets	✓
Liabilities	.

C = A − L

(2 marks)

You have identified several transactions that are Amy's personal expenditure, rather than for Catering for Occasions. You tell her you cannot include these in the financial statements for Catering for Occasions under accounting principles.

(b)   Which is the relevant accounting principle for removing Amy's personal transactions?

Tick the correct option.

Prudence	
Going concern	
Business entity	✓
Materiality	

(1 mark)

Amy purchased a new van on 1 January 20-5 for £25,000. She expects to use it in her business for five years and anticipates it will have a value at the end of this period of £5,000.

(c)   Using the straight-line method of depreciation, calculate the depreciation charge for the year ended 31 December 20-5.

£ **4,000**

(1 mark)

25,000 − 5,000 = 20,000

20,000 ÷ 5 = 4,000

When the new van was purchased, Amy part-exchanged the old van against it for £3,200. This disposal has not yet been accounted for. The old van cost £16,000 and has accumulated depreciation of £14,100 on 1 January 20-5. No depreciation is charged in the year of disposal.

(d) Calculate the profit or loss on disposal of the old van, and indicate if it will be a debit or credit to the statement of profit or loss.

£ ⬚ 1,300   ▨ Credit

16,000 − 14,100 = 1,900

(1 mark)

Catering for Occasions operates no special accounting schemes. One of its regular customers was invoiced on 15 March 20-5 for a birthday party for £2,100, plus VAT, and was offered one month's credit. Subsequently the customer has refused to pay, as he stated the food and service was not of an acceptable standard. Amy decided to write off the debt on 1 October 20-5. All the conditions for bad debt relief apply.

(e) What is the earliest opportunity for the business to claim bad debt relief? Tick the correct option.

In its VAT period ended 31 March 20-5	
In its VAT period ended 31 December 20-5	✓
In its VAT period ended 30 June 20-6	

(1 mark)

Just prior to the year end, Amy catered for a large wedding party which generated sales of £5,000 excluding VAT. She raised an invoice for the deposit of 50% on 16 December 20-4, which was paid on 31 December 20-4. She raised the final invoice on 21 December 20-5, and it was paid on 30 December 20-5.

(f) When was the tax point for the deposit and the final invoice? Tick the correct option.

16 December 20-4 and 30 December 20-5	
21 December 20-5 and 21 December 20-5	
16 December 20-4 and 21 December 20-5	✓

(2 marks)

Amy is considering moving over to the annual accounting scheme for VAT.

(g) Complete the following statement. Choose the correct options.

During the year the trader must pay ▨ 90% ▨ of the estimated annual VAT liability in nine equal instalments.

(1 mark)

You have also been working on the management accounts. Amy's budgeted food sales for 20-5 were based on catering for 6,360 people, at an average sales price of £15 per head.

(h)   **(i)**   Calculate the food sales budget for 20-5.

£ | 95,400

(1 mark)

Actual food sales in 20-5 were £103,648 and a total of 6,560 people were catered for.

(ii)   Calculate the flexed food budget and the sales price variance for 20-5. Show an adverse variance as negative.

	£
Flexed food sales budget	
Sales price variance	

(2 marks)

You have been reviewing the trial balance and are aware that certain accounts can have either a debit or a credit balance.

(i)   Which two of the following accounts can have a debit or credit balance in the general ledger? Select the correct options.

Irrecoverable debts expense	
Petty cash	
VAT account	
Capital	

(2 marks)

Amy has recently started providing a catered hot lunch for 60 staff at a local company whose canteen is being refurbished. Amy hired additional equipment for the contract period, which runs from 1 December 20-5 to 28 February 20-6. The equipment hire cost £960 and was invoiced on 12 December 20-5. You must account for the hire of this equipment in the financial statements for the year ended 31 December 20-5.

(j) Complete the statement below. Select from the following options: an accrued expense, a prepaid expense, £320, £640, £960.

The financial statements will include an amount of | £ [   ] | for [   ] .

(2 marks)

You are reviewing the repairs and maintenance account in the financial statements and are concerned that the figure is high. On closer inspection, you realise a new mixer costing £900 has been miscoded and has been incorrectly included in the repairs and maintenance account. Items above £500 are usually capitalised.

(k) Identify two consequences of the miscoding of the mixer. Select the two correct options.

Profit will be overstated	
Profit will be understated	
Non-current assets will be understated	
Depreciation will be overstated	

(2 marks)

You are doing some checks on the year-end figures and have calculated the total sales of the business in 20-5 to be £111,250. You think some cost information is missing, so need to calculate the cost of sales. Amy earns a gross profit margin of 45% on each job.

(l) **(i)** Calculate the cost of sales for 20-5 to the nearest £.

£ [   ]

(1 mark)

Amy is considering using mark-up in 20-6, instead of margin, to prepare quotes to customers.

(ii) Amy currently bases her sales price on achieving a gross profit margin of 45%. If she decides to use mark-up in 20-6, identify whether the mark-up percentage would be higher or lower than the 45% gross margin currently used.

Mark-up percentage would be lower than the gross profit percentage	
Mark-up percentage would be higher than the gross profit percentage	

(1 mark)

Task 2: 10 marks

Catering for Occasions currently uses a manual accounting system, maintaining manual daybooks and control accounts. It is considering using accounting software.

(a)   Choose which two of the following statements are true regarding accounting software.

It will automatically ensure all transactions are entered with the correct date	
It will transfer information from the sales and purchases daybooks into the relevant control account automatically	
It will automate the period end routine	
It will determine whether transactions are genuine, so should be included in the accounts	

(2 marks)

(b)   Complete the following statement regarding the year end processes carried out by accounting software. Select from the following options: statement of profit or loss, statement of financial position.

Accounting software will automatically balance off and create a brought forward balance for items that are included on the [   ].

(1 mark)

Ted, one of Amy's clients, has suggested that Amy does not raise an invoice for the catering for his birthday party, and that he pays her in cash. He has explained that this would mean he would not have to pay VAT, making the party cheaper for him, and she would benefit from not paying the tax on the profit she makes on the party.

Amy has told your colleague, Sarah, who also works in accounts, that she intends to do this and has promised to share the tax she saves with Sarah.

(c) If you ignore this incorrect treatment of sales and consequent unpayment of tax, what offence could you be accused of? Select the correct option.

Tipping off / Failure to disclose / Tax evasion

(1 mark)

Amy is considering whether she should improve the sustainability of her business. She has asked you to clarify what sustainability is.

(d)   Which of the following statements describes the meaning of sustainability? Tick the correct option.

Ensuring the short-term needs of the organisation are prioritised over its long-term needs	
Allowing the needs of future generations to be met without compromising the ability of future generations to meet their own needs	
Promoting the use of local suppliers to improve sales	

(1 mark)

Now that Amy understands sustainability better, she has decided to run her business more sustainably. She has asked you to review the current working practices below to determine if they support sustainability or not.

(e)   Which two of the following working practices support sustainability? Tick the correct options.

Pricing jobs to include paying staff a living wage, rather than the legal minimum wage	
Renegotiating with food suppliers every year to get the best price	
Ensuring fridges and freezers are replaced with the most energy saving models	
Throwing excess food away at the end of each job	

(2 marks)

You have been asked to help prepare payroll reports. A colleague has asked you what a P11D form is used for.

(f)   **(i)**   Choose the option that describes what a P11D form is used for.

A summary of payroll information to date when an employee leaves	
A form showing any benefits in kind an employee has received during the year	
The tax an employee has paid during the tax year	

(1 mark)

(ii) For the tax year ending 5 April 20-6, when does the P11D form have to be submitted to HMRC by?
Select the correct option.

5 April 20-6	
6 July 20-6	
22 July 20-6	

(1 mark)

Amy is aware that Catering for Occasions must comply with data protection regulations for both customers and employees. She has asked you to clarify the principles of data protection for her.

(g) Identify the option that includes three principles of data protection. Tick the correct option.

Transparency, accuracy, and accountability	
Comprehensive data, integrity and confidentiality, storage limitation	
Lawfulness, fairness and responsibility	

(1 mark)

Task 3: 10 marks

You have been asked to assist in some reconciliations.

You have reconciled the inventory records to the physical inventory and found several differences. Which two items below would be adjusted in the inventory account in the general ledger?

(a)   Identify the two items that will require an adjustment in the inventory account in the general ledger. Tick the correct options.

Damaged inventory, previously recorded at no value, has been disposed of	
Items have been despatched to a customer but the inventory records have not been updated	
Goods that have been received into inventory were not recorded	
Customer returns that have been included in the physical inventory count	

(2 marks)

The non-current assets on the non-current asset register have been physically inspected and the register has been updated. It has then been compared to the non-current asset: cost account in the general ledger.

The non-current asset: cost account in the general ledger has a balance of £39,230. However, the non-current asset register shows assets with a total cost of £33,500. You have been asked to explain the difference.

(b)   Which two of the following reasons could result in the balance on the non-current asset: cost account in the general ledger being higher than the non-current asset register? Tick the correct options.

The disposal of two old freezers has not been recorded in the general ledger	
The purchase of two new heat boxes for £500 was recorded in the asset register as £1,000	
A food mixer costing £799 has been stolen	
The owner purchased an old fridge from the business for personal use for £100. The profit on disposal in the disposal account was £20.	

(2 marks)

At the beginning of the month, the outstanding balance on the payables ledger control account was £6,463. During the month, food and drink purchases on credit were £3,643. Some of the items were of poor quality, so were returned. The business received a credit note for £78. Sales on credit to business customers in the month were £11,240. Customers were offered a 3% prompt payment discount, and all paid early to have it. There were no other transactions in the month.

(c)   Calculate the balance on the payables ledger control account at the end of the month.

£ [   ]

(1 mark)

You have been asked to investigate a credit balance on the suspense account of £52.

(d)   If corrected, which error could clear the suspense account? Select the correct option.

A wages payment made using petty cash which did not have a petty cash slip to support it	
A sundry cash sale received into petty cash but with no petty cash slip created to record it	

(1 mark)

You are completing the bank reconciliation as at 31 March 20-6. You have compared the cash book and the bank statement and found the following issues. You now need to update the cash book for some items.

(e)   Which two of the following items need to be updated in the cash book? Select the correct options.

(a) A faster payment of £375 has been recorded in the cash book as £275	
(b) A cheque paid to a supplier for £340 has cleared the bank on 5 April 20-6	
(c) Overdraft charges of £31 have not been entered into the cash book	
(d) A customer remittance was received, dated 30 March 20-6, and entered into the cash book. The payment has not yet been received	

(2 marks)

Amy is unclear why a business should reconcile the bank account to the cash book every month.

(f)   Why do businesses reconcile the bank account to the cash book on a regular basis? Tick the correct option.

To keep track of the bank balance each period	
To make sure the bank is applying the correct bank charges	
To ensure the cash book accurately reflects the bank transactions of the business	

(1 mark)

You have just learned about 'professional scepticism' in your studies. When you reviewed sales for April 20-6 you find that Amy has personally raised several sales invoices for which there are no purchase invoices and no staff costs related to them.

(g)   If you are applying professional scepticism to this situation, which of these reasons must you consider for Amy raising these invoices? Select the correct option.

Amy is behind in her paperwork for purchases and wages in April	
Amy wants to overstate profit in April	
Amy wants to understate profit in April	

(1 mark)

Practice knowledge assessment 3

Assessment information

Complete all three tasks.

There are 40 marks in the assessment.

Where the date is relevant, it is given in the task data.

Both minus signs and brackets can be used to indicate negative numbers unless the task instructions say otherwise.

Advice

Read each question carefully before you start to answer it.

Attempt all questions. In the exam, the questions will be computer-marked.

You will have 2 hours and 30 minutes to answer all parts of the assessment. This includes 90 minutes for the assessment and a further 60 minutes for reflection and planning as needed.

Task 1: 20 marks

You work at Goodenough & Co, a medium sized accountancy firm, which provides accountancy services for many clients including Owen & Sons, a firm of builders, owned by Oscar Owen.

You are currently preparing the year-end financial records and statements for Owen & Sons for the period ended 31 March 20-7. You are aware it relies on an overdraft from the bank to help it manage short-term cash flow problems. If Oscar Owen is unable to renew the business overdraft, what accounting principle might require adjustments in the financial statements?

(a)   Identify which accounting principle might require Owen & Sons financial statements to be adjusted if the overdraft is not renewed. Select the correct option.

Prudence	
Accruals	
Going concern	

(1 mark)

On 1 February 20-7, Owen & Sons purchased a smaller digger on hire purchase to use on its building jobs. You have been given the following information about the purchase.

	£
Cost of digger	9,200
Delivery charges	300
Annual insurance	250

(b)   **(i)**   Calculate the figure that should be recorded as capital expenditure in the financial statements.

£ [   ]

(1 mark)

(ii)   Complete the following statement. Choose the correct option.

The purchase of the new digger will **increase / decrease** the assets on the statement of financial position.

(1 mark)

Owen & Sons is in dispute with a customer over an extension it built in 20-6. Oscar Owen, the owner, considers the business may have to pay £5,300 to the customer in May 20-7 to settle the dispute. This potential payment to the customer must be included in the financial statements for year ended 31 March 20-7.

(c)   How should the potential payment to the customer be included in the financial statements for year ended 31 March 20-7? Select the correct option.

Accrued expenses	
Prepaid expenses	
Accrued income	
Prepaid income	

(1 mark)

Oscar Owen has told you that the business purchased some materials for £3,600 plus VAT on 16 March 20-7, from a builder that has now ceased trading. You have not been given an invoice for the purchase, and Oscar wants you to include it in the financial statements for the year ended 31 March 20-7.

(d)   Which qualitative characteristic will **not** be complied with if you include the purchase of £3,600?

Select the correct option.

Timeliness	
Verifiability	
Relevance	

(1 mark)

Oscar Owen wants to reduce the amount of paperwork in his office so is planning to scan his accounting records and store them electronically.

(e)   Under accounting rules, Oscar is allowed to store accounting records electronically. True or False?

True / False

(1 mark)

You are now working on another client, Excellence in Recruitment. You provide payroll services to the client and are currently working on this month's salaries. Excellence in Recruitment has a pension scheme which its employees can choose to pay into. It also facilitates employees to donate to charities through their pay. Some of its employees have student loans and there is the option for staff to pay for private health insurance.

You are reviewing the taxable pay for employees for this month, and considering items which reduce gross pay to taxable pay.

(f)   Identify which items reduce gross pay to find taxable pay. Tick all the correct options.

Charitable donations	
Pension contributions	
Private healthcare	
Student loans	

(2 marks)

Toni, the owner of Excellence in Recruitment, has asked you to confirm the date statutory deductions must be paid to HMRC for salary payments made on 31 July 20-7.

(g)   **(i)**   Identify the date statutory deductions should be paid to HMRC for monthly salaries paid on 31 July 20-7. Tick the correct option.

31 July 20-7	
19 August 20-7	
22 August 20-7	
31 August 20-7	

(1 mark)

Toni has already been late paying amounts due for payroll to HMRC three times this tax year and has indicated this month's payment will also be late. She is aware she will attract penalties from HMRC because of this.

(ii) Identify the number of defaults the business will have, and the penalty percentage that will be applied to the amount that is late, if she pays late a fourth time. Tick the correct option.

Two defaults and 1%	
Three defaults and 1%	
Three defaults and 2%	
Four defaults and 2%	

(1 mark)

Toni is considering raising finance to grow Excellence in Recruitment and needs to know whether she should produce monthly management accounts. She has asked you why she should produce them.

(h) **(i)** Identify a reason for Toni's business, Excellence in Recruitment, to produce management accounts. Select one option.

To enable Excellence in Recruitment to meet its legal obligations	
To assist in planning the timing and value of resources required by Excellence in Recruitment	
To allow Toni to determine her dividend payments	

(1 mark)

You have produced the management accounts for Excellence in Recruitment for the month of September 20-7.

(ii) Calculate the labour variance for July 20-7 and indicate if it is adverse or favourable.

	Budget £	Actual £	Variance £	Adverse / favourable
Labour cost	11,500	12,325		

(1 marks)

(iii)   Identify a possible reason for this labour variance. Select the correct option.

The planned employment of a new recruitment consultant was delayed for one month	
A new client management system was introduced in September 20-7	
An additional administrator started in September 20-7, which was not planned for	
A bonus, allowed for in the budget, was paid in September 20-7	

(1 mark)

You are now working on the year-end accounts for another client, Able & Best, a fruit farm, and are preparing the light & heat account. The account has an opening debit balance of £6,420. The cash book figure for the year is £82,340.

(i)   Complete the light & heat expense account, ensuring it is balanced off appropriately. Complete the figures and select from the following options to describe each entry: balance b/d, balance c/d, cash book, statement of profit or loss

	£		£

(3 marks)

You have noticed that the trade payables figure on Able & Best's trial balance is difference to the total of the payables accounts balances in the memorandum accounts.

(j)   Identify which of the following could be a reason for this difference. Select the correct option.

A credit note has been allocated to the wrong supplier	
An invoice has been allocated to the wrong supplier's account	
A bank payment has been allocated to the wrong supplier	
A bank payment has been allocated to the wrong nominal code	

(1 mark)

You have reviewed Able & Best's trial balance. Although the trial balance balances, it includes a bank receipt that has been incorrectly posted. Cash from fruit picking sales that was paid into the bank has been entered as £560 but should have been entered as £650.

(k)   Calculate the amount to be posted to the bank account to correct this error.

£

(1 mark)

In Able & Best's accounts for the year ended 30 June 20-7, you must now account for prepaid deposits received for holiday lets on the fruit farm for stays after 1 July 20-7.

(l)   Complete the following sentence. Select from the following options: an asset, a liability.

Prepaid income will be shown as [   ] in the statement of financial position.

(1 mark)

Task 2: 10 marks

Daisy, a trainee at Goodenough & Co, is currently working with you on the financial statements for a local builder, Owen & Sons. She has asked you about stakeholders and wants to understand the difference between internal and external stakeholders.

(a)   Complete the following statement, selecting from the following options: external, internal.

The customers of Owen & Sons are [   ] stakeholders, whilst the employees are

[   ] stakeholders.

(1 mark)

You are now working on the financial statements of Leominster Fabrications Ltd. You have identified a cash receipt of £1,300 which has been recorded as the proceeds from the sale of some equipment. This was paid into the business bank account by the Managing Director. You cannot find any record of the purchase of the equipment, and you suspect money laundering.

(b)   **(i)**   Complete the following statement. Select from these options: layering, placement, integration.

This is an example of [   ] .

(1 mark)

(ii)   If you do not report this possible money laundering offence, what could a consequence be for you? Select one option.

Nothing – the amount is below the financial limit for reporting money laundering activities	
You could be prosecuted for failure to report and fined and/or sent to prison for up to five years	
You could be prosecuted for failure to report and fined and/or sent to prison for up to 14 years	

(1 mark)

(iii)   Who would you report the suspicious activity to? Choose the correct option.

The National Crime Agency	
The Managing Director of Leominster Fabrications	
The Money Laundering Reporting Officer	

(1 mark)

(iv)   Complete the following statement, selecting from the following options: a protected disclosure, an authorised disclosure.

If you have not engaged in money laundering, when you report the money laundering activity, you are making [   ] .

(1 mark)

You are now working on the quarterly VAT Return for Able & Best, a fruit farm that supplies local supermarkets, lets holiday cottages, and runs a 'pick your own fruit' operation. It supplies both zero-rated and standard-rated VAT supplies.

(c)   **(i)**   Identify which of these is the definition of a zero-rated VAT supply. Select the correct option.

Supplies that are taxed at 0%	
Supplies that are taxed at the standard VAT rate	
Supplies on which VAT is not chargeable	

(1 mark)

(ii)   Given that Able & Best supplies both zero-rated and standard-rated supplies, how much of the input tax on purchases will Able & Best be able to reclaim?

All of the input tax	
A proportion of the input tax	
None of the input tax	

(1 mark)

On 1 July 20-6, the balance on Able & Best's allowance for doubtful receivables account was £2,176. On 30 June 20-7, the balance on the receivables ledger was £79,569. Able & Best expects 5% of these receivables not to pay.

(d)   **(i)**   Calculate the adjustment required at 30 June 20-7 to the allowances for doubtful receivables account to the nearest £.

£ [   ]

(1 mark)

(ii)   Complete the journal to record the change in the allowance for doubtful receivables, indicating
if it is a debit or a credit. Select from the following options: Allowance for doubtful receivables;
Allowance for doubtful receivables: adjustment; Irrecoverable debt.

Account	Debit / Credit

(2 marks)

Task 3: 10 marks

You have been asked to assist in resolving some queries for clients.

Owen & Sons has a non-current asset register which is maintained on a spreadsheet. Oscar Owen, the owner has some questions about the non-current register.

(a)   Identify whether the statements below are true or false regarding non-current asset registers. Tick the correct option.

Statement	True / False
(a) The non-current asset register must be reconciled to the nominal ledger to ensure the non-current assets are accurately recorded in the accounts	
(b) Non-current assets do not need to be physically compared to the non-current asset register each period	

(2 marks)

Oscar Owen has reviewed the financial statements for Owen & Sons for the year ended 31 March 20-7 and would like to know what is included in cost of sales in the statement of profit or loss.

(b)   Which of the following formulas shows the correct calculation for cost of sales in the statement of profit or loss? Tick the correct formula.

Opening inventory plus purchases plus closing inventory	
Opening inventory less purchases less closing inventory	
Opening inventory plus purchases less closing inventory	
Opening inventory less purchases plus closing inventory	

(1 mark)

Oscar Owen has accidentally purchased items for Owen & Sons with his personal credit card, rather than using the business credit card.

(c)   **(i)**   Identify whether each of the following items is capital expenditure or revenue expenditure. Select the correct option.

Payment made by Oscar Owen	Capital or Revenue
Wood and plasterboard costing £3,900 for refurbishing a customer's house	
A new hammer drill costing £2,300 to replace the previous drill which was purchased several years ago	

(2 marks)

(ii)   Which elements of the financial statements of Owen & Sons will increase when the capital items purchased using Oscar Owen's personal credit card are recorded? Tick the correct options.

Assets	
Liabilities	
Capital	

(2 marks)

You are now working on the financial statements of Gym-mine, an online business selling personalised gym equipment, including clothing and health monitoring equipment. The business has used Goodenough & Co as its accountants since it was founded.

The business has been growing for several years and now uses social media to promote itself. It generates a large volume of business transactions each day and is in the process of upgrading its website.

The owner of Gym-mine, Molly Fox, has been told by the web design company Gym-mine uses that the new website will be able to process big data. Molly has asked you to help clarify her understanding of big data.

(d)   **(i)**   Which of the following options is a source of big data? Select the correct option.

Transitional data	
Society data	
Machine data	

(1 mark)

Big data has a number of characteristics.

    (ii)   Which one of the following characteristics of big data is correctly explained? Select the correct option.

Velocity: data obtained from different sources, both internal and external	
Veracity: data that is truthful, trustworthy, and accurate	
Value: data that relates to financial, numerical values	

    (1 mark)

Gym-mine produces the accounts using accounting software. The current website automatically enters information into the software for sales and receipts. Several new products are added each month and the website is updated for these.

(e)   Identify if the following statement is true or false.

    The entries entered by the website into the accounting software will always be accurate, so do not need to be checked.

    True / False

    (1 mark)

Practice knowledge assessment 4

Assessment information

Complete all three tasks.

There are 40 marks in the assessment.

Where the date is relevant, it is given in the task data.

Both minus signs and brackets can be used to indicate negative numbers unless the task instructions say otherwise.

Advice

Read each question carefully before you start to answer it.

Attempt all questions. In the exam, the questions will be computer-marked.

You will have 2 hours and 30 minutes to answer all parts of the assessment. This includes 90 minutes for the assessment and a further 60 minutes for reflection and planning as needed.

Task 1: 20 marks

You are an accounts assistant for Beautiful Tableware, a business owned by Clare. You are preparing the year-end financial records and statements for the period ended 31 March 20-5. You have been asked to prepare a number of transactions and record them in the accounting records. You also need to make some corrections.

(a) You have been asked to determine which of the items below, included in the financial statements, supports the prudence concept. Select the correct option.

Including only transactions relating to the business	
Valuing inventory at the lower of cost and net realisable value	
Including electricity costs for production in cost of sales	
Capitalising machinery with a cost of £500, or more	

(1 mark)

Whilst reviewing the non-current asset register, you realise that a new lorry, included in motor vehicles, has been included on the non-current asset register and general ledger for £36,000, including VAT. However, VAT is reclaimable on lorries. Consequently, the value of the lorry included on the non-current asset register and the general ledger is incorrect.

(b) If you correct this error in the non-current asset register and the general ledger, what will the impact be on the depreciation charge for the year?

Increase the depreciation charge	
Decrease the depreciation charge	
No change to the depreciation charge	

(1 mark)

You have been asked to update the non-current asset register for a disposal. The owner, Clare, bought a car on 1 April 20-3 for £17,500. Since then it has been depreciated at 25% per year using the diminishing balance method. The company policy is to charge a full year's depreciation in both the year of acquisition and the year of disposal. The car was sold on 1 January 20-5.

(c) **(i)** Calculate the depreciation charge for the year ended 31 March 20-4.

£ [　　　　　　　]

(1 mark)

(ii)   Calculate the profit or loss on disposal of the car and indicate if it is a profit or a loss.

£ [ ]   profit / loss

(2 marks)

Clare is considering how to fund the purchase of a new car for one of the sales staff. Beautiful Tableware does not want to use current monies to fund the purchase.

(d)   Which one the following funding methods would you suggest it uses?

Cash purchase	
Purchase on 30 days credit terms	
Bank overdraft	
Hire purchase	

(1 mark)

You have reviewed the VAT Return for the period ended 31 December 20-4 and realise there are two non-deliberate and non-careless errors made. Sales for this quarter, excluding VAT, are £75,250.

• A sales invoice for £15,000, including VAT, was incorrectly excluded from the accounting records.

• On 31 December 20-4 a new customer paid a deposit of £28,000, excluding VAT, for a new, personalised line the business is making exclusively for the customer. Beautiful Tableware has issued a receipt but no invoice, as it will raise this on completion of the work in April 20-5.

(e)   **(i)**   Calculate the additional VAT that needs to be corrected on this VAT Return.

£ [ ]

(2 marks)

(ii)   Complete the following sentence. Select the correct options.

To correct this error, Beautiful Tableware will need to **add this figure to / subtract this figure from** the **output tax / input tax** figure on the current VAT Return.

(2 marks)

Clare has just received a large order for a one-off batch of Beautiful Tableware's stoneware. She has partially completed the cost card below and wants you to complete the direct costs. She has given you the following information:

- Each batch uses 240 kgs of materials, costing £4.30 per kg

- It takes a skilled worker, that costs £18.50 per hour, eight minutes to produce each dish

(f)   **(i)**   Complete the direct materials and labour cost for the batch of dishes on the cost card below, and calculate the total cost of the batch.

Cost card for 600 x 60cm Stoneware circular dish	
	£
Direct materials	
Direct labour	
Production overheads	5,470
Total cost of batch	

(2 marks)

You have been given the following information relating to the insurance.

- On 31 March 20-4 an entry of £1,690 was made into the insurance account for prepaid insurance. This entry needs to be reversed in the current year.

- Cash book entries for the current year relating to insurance are £6,700. This includes a payment of £2,292 which relates to the period 1 January 20-5 to 31 December 20-5.

(g)   **(i)**   Identify what type of adjustment is required on the insurance account on 31 March 20-5. Select the correct option.

Prepaid expenses	
Prepaid incomes	
Accrued expenses	
Accrued incomes	

(1 mark)

(ii) Complete and balance off the insurance account.

Select from the following options: Prepaid expenses reversal, Balance b/d, Balance c/d, Cash book, Accrued expenses, Insurance, Purchases, Statement of profit or loss, Prepaid expenses.

Insurance account			
	£		£
Total		Total	

(3 marks)

The balance on the receivables ledger control account as at 31 March 20-5 is £35,460. Clare has historically made an allowance for doubtful receivables equal to 4% of trade receivables.

The company has one general ledger account that contains specific and general allowances for doubtful receivables. On 1 April 20-4, the balance on this account was £1,808.

Clare asked you to make an allowance for a specific debt of £3,120, invoiced in December 20-4, which she considers is now unlikely to be paid.

(h) Produce journal entries relating to the allowance for doubtful receivables as at 31 March 20-5 to the nearest penny. The specific and general allowances should be journaled separately.

Select from: Allowance for doubtful receivables; Allowance for doubtful receivables: adjustment; Irrecoverable debt; Receivables ledger control account; Sales revenue; Statement of profit or loss.

Account	Debit £	Credit £

(4 marks)

Task 2: 10 marks

Clare wants to improve the information used to run Beautiful Tableware. She has asked you what turns data it holds into useful information for the business.

(a)   Identify two attributes of good quality information from the choices below. Select two options.

Complex	
Complete	
Defined	
Authoritative	

(2 marks)

Clare has asked you to help her present the sales data, by product, for the last two years, to the bank, in order to help secure a loan. Sales have grown by 25% in 20-5 compared with 20-4, and Clare wants to highlight this in a suitable graph.

(b)   Identify the most appropriate type of graph to present this information from the options below.

Matrix chart	
Pie chart	
Column chart	
Doughnut chart	

(1 mark)

Clare is considering introducing a new computerised accounting system that could be used to present information to senior managers in the business using a weekly dashboard.

(c)   Identify two benefits of presenting information in a dashboard.

Visual information can be easier for non-financial managers to understand than tables	
Only relevant data is displayed	
A standard dashboard can be used	
The dashboard can include comprehensive, detailed information to cover every aspect of the business	
The dashboard can be updated to include real-time data	

(2 marks)

You currently use a manual system for recording accounting entries.

(d)   Identify whether each of the following statements is true or false for a manual accounting system. Select the correct option.

Statement	True	False
A trial balance produced using a manual system will always balance		
A manual system cannot use daybooks to summarise transactions to post to the general ledger		
The receivables ledger control account will automatically agree to the receivables ledger in a manual system		

(3 marks)

You have been asked to balance off several general ledger accounts, as part of the year end.

(e)   Select the type of accounts that will include a balance carried down at the end of the financial year. Tick the correct options.

Motor vehicles	
Interest payable	
Depreciation charge	
Accrued expenses	

(2 marks)

Task 3: 10 marks

You have been asked to assist with some reconciliations, as well as resolving some errors in the accounts.

On 1 February 20-5, Clare purchased a laptop and printer for use in the business using her personal credit card. She would like you to record them in the financial statements. The VAT on the invoice is reclaimable.

An extract of the invoice is shown below:

Description	Amount £
HK Pavilion Laptop 17"	550.30
Canon Printer TX89	140.65
Printer cartridges	50.00
Delivery	19.99
Total Net Amount	760.94
VAT @ 20%	152.18
Total gross Amount	913.12

(a)   **(i)**   Calculate the cost to be included in non-current assets for the transaction.

£ [ ]

(1 mark)

(ii)   Indicate the impact of the transaction on the following elements of the accounting equation.

Element	Increase	Decrease	No change
Assets			
Liabilities			
Capital			

(3 marks)

You are investigating an error in the financial statements, relating to a bank payment to a supplier.

(b) Complete the following sentence. Indicate the correct option.

A bank payment made to PL Materials Ltd for £11,987 has been debited in the payables ledger to the account for LP Materials Ltd. This means the trial balance **will / will not** balance.

(1 mark)

You have now been asked to investigate the suspense account with a balance of £540 debit.

(c) Once corrected, which error could clear the suspense account? Select the correct option.

The sales returns daybook, totalling £1,714, was entered into the receivables ledger control account as £1,174	
The sales daybook, totalling £1,714, was entered into the receivables ledger control account as £1,174	

(1 mark)

On 31 March 20-5, the bank statement shows a debit balance of £1,650 and the cash book shows a debit balance of £926. The cash book currently shows outstanding lodgements of £2,513. The cash book and bank account do not currently reconcile, but you have identified the missing item.

(d) Which one of the following items will reconcile the cash book and the bank statement? Tick the correct option.

A BACS receipt from a customer not yet recorded in the cash book of £63	
A BACS receipt from a customer for £3,237 not yet recorded in the cash book	
Bank charges of £63 not yet recorded in the cash book	
An unpresented cheque of £3,237 which has not cleared the bank	

(1 mark)

You have reconciled the inventory records to the physical inventory and, as a result, the value of closing inventory in the financial statements should be reduced by £27,900. Before this adjustment, the profit for the year is £21,600. Clare has suggested that you do not adjust the closing inventory value, as she is looking to attract further investment in the business from the bank.

(e) What action should you take regarding the inventory adjustment? Tick one option.

Do not adjust the inventory value, as Clare is the owner of the business, so she is responsible for the financial statements	
Explain to Clare that the inventory value should be correct to comply with accounting regulations	
Offer to resign if she will not amend the financial statements	

(1 mark)

Clare has recently undertaken a review of raw materials purchases. She has found a new overseas supplier for clay that will charge 20% less than her current UK supplier. Which of these working practices would indicate that the potential new supplier works sustainably?

(f) From the options below, identify one sustainable working practice that should be in place at the new supplier. Tick the correct option.

The supplier is pricing to ensure it is highly profitable	
The supplier's employees are working in safe conditions	
The supplier's transport costs are low and cost-effective	

(1 mark)

You have just noticed a large deposit made into the bank account by Clare with no supporting documentation. You suspect money laundering, and must now send a suspicious activity report to the National Crime Agency.

(g) If it is available, what information must be included in the suspicious activity report? Select the correct option.

The whereabouts of the laundered property	
The passport number of the suspected money launderer	
The tax number of the suspected money launderer	

(1 mark)

Practice knowledge assessment 5

Assessment information

Complete all three tasks.

There are 40 marks in the assessment.

Where the date is relevant, it is given in the task data.

Both minus signs and brackets can be used to indicate negative numbers unless the task instructions say otherwise.

Advice

Read each question carefully before you start to answer it.

Attempt all questions. In the exam, the questions will be computer-marked.

You will have 2 hours and 30 minutes to answer all parts of the assessment. This includes 90 minutes for the assessment and a further 60 minutes for reflection and planning, as needed.

Task 1: 20 marks

You work as the accountant for Trendy Togs, a clothing business owned by Luke Graham.

You are currently reviewing some suppliers' accounts. You have realised that VAT on a credit note received by the business includes VAT of £85, but this should have been £58. Currently, the VAT control account includes output tax of £7,535 and input tax of £2,135.

(a)   **(i)**   Calculate the amended balance on the VAT control account.

£ [   ]

(1 mark)

(ii)   Complete the following statement:

The balance on the VAT control account will be a **debit / credit**.

(1 mark)

Luke Graham has sold £75 of zero-rated children's clothes and standard-rated adult clothes for £100, plus VAT of £20, to a customer.

(b)   What will the balance be on the simplified VAT invoice issued by Trendy Togs to the customer? Select the correct option.

£75	
£100	
£175	
£195	

(1 mark)

You have reconciled the VAT account and then produced the VAT Return for the quarter ended 31 March 20-6. By what date must this VAT Return be submitted to HMRC?

(c)   When must the VAT Return be submitted to HMRC for the quarter ended 31 March 20-6? Select the correct option.

30 April 20-6	
7 April 20-6	
10 April 20-6	

(1 mark)

Luke has asked you why you need to carry out so many reconciliations as a part of the production of the financial statements. Which qualitative characteristic requires you to complete these reconciliations?

(d)   Identify the qualitative characteristic that requires you to reconcile balances in the financial statements. Tick the correct option.

Relevance	
Comparability	
Faithful representation	

(1 mark)

You are producing the period end adjustments for vehicles costs for the year. On 31 March 20-5, an accrual of £500 for vehicles costs was made. During the year, vehicle costs of £4,200 were paid for through the bank, including one bank payment of £120 for road tax for the year from 1 April 20-6 to 31 March 20-7.

(e)   **(i)**   Calculate the amount to be included in the statement of profit or loss for the year ended 31 March 20-6 for vehicle costs.

£ [   ]

(1 mark)

(ii)   Complete the following sentence.

The **prepaid expenses / accrued expenses** for vehicle costs for the road tax will be reversed on **31 March 20-6 / 1 April 20-6.**

(2 marks)

Recently, Luke Graham has been very busy, so has not kept the accounting information up to date. He has asked you to estimate the gross profit for the year ended 31 March 20-6. He has given you the following information:

- Luke applies an average gross profit margin of 60%

- Net sales for the year are £220,000

- Opening inventory is £24,000

- Net purchases for the year, excluding VAT, are £90,000

(f)   Calculate the estimated gross profit and cost of sales figures for the year ended 31 March 20-6.

	£
Gross profit	
Cost of sales	

(2 marks)

Luke has now completed the inventory count and has asked you to value the following items to include in the closing inventory valuation.

(g)   Calculate the value for each item of inventory in the table below.

	Quantity £	Cost £	Selling price £	Inventory value £
Marble-pattern dress, size 16	2	18.99	39.99	
Lounge trousers, 38" waist 34" leg	3	29.99	19.99	

(2 marks)

Trendy Togs is growing, so you have suggested the business introduces budgeting for the following year.

(h)   Identify the key reason Trendy Togs should introduce budgeting. Select the correct option.

Budgeting will enable the business to monitor actual sales by product	
Budgeting can improve the control and decision making in the business	
Budgeting will ensure the business makes more profit by monitoring costs closely	

(1 mark)

You are using the financial information for the year ended 31 March 20-6 to produce a budget for the year ended 31 March 20-7. Actual sales for the year ended 31 March 20-6 are £220,000, and Luke anticipates sales to grow by 75% next year. How much should the revenue budget be for year ended 31 March 20-7?

(i) Calculate the sales revenue budget for the year ended 31 March 20-7.

£ [   ]

(1 mark)

Luke Graham, the owner of Trendy Togs, has asked you which type of budget is most suitable for the business. He hopes to grow sales by 75% and expects to be able to do this using the same shop and staff, and by introducing new clothing lines. Despite these plans, Luke is uncertain about his revenue forecast. He wants to amend his budget on a monthly basis to allow for the changes in sales levels.

(j) Identify the most suitable type of budget Trendy Togs should use to monitor actual results against budget in the next financial year.

Fixed budget	
Flexed budget	
Rolling budget	

(1 mark)

Luke has asked you to calculate the wages budget for the shop for next year. He employs a part-time manager who earns £17,500 per annum, and another staff member for 30 hours per week at £16 per hour.

(k) Calculate the total wages budget for the shop for the year ended 31 March 20-7.

£ [   ]

(1 mark)

Luke has recently renovated the shop. He purchased a new display rail costing £200, excluding VAT. He has created a new changing room at a cost of £1,500 and the shop has been repainted at a cost of £2,100. The capitalisation policy for the business is set for items over £250.

(l) **(i)** How much of the shop renovation can be capitalised? Tick the correct option.

£1,500	
£1,700	
£3,600	
£3,800	

(1 mark)

(ii) What impact does capitalisation have on the statement of profit or loss? Tick the correct option.

When an item is capitalised, the expenses in the statement of profit or loss increase	
When an item is not capitalised, the expenses in the statement of profit or loss increase	

(1 mark)

Luke has asked you why he needs to have a capitalisation policy that means items under £250, such as the clothes rail, are not included in non-current assets.

(iii) Identify which one of the following options explains why this policy appropriate.

The principle of materiality means that the users' view of the financial statements will not change if small items are not capitalised	
It is not worth the time and effort to maintain a non-current asset register with lots of low value items	
A company is not allowed to capitalise everything in its financial statements	

(1 mark)

Trendy Togs has several regular customers who buy on credit, so you maintain a manual sales daybook and receivables ledger. In March 20-6, Paula Patel purchased goods for £2,100, which included VAT of £350. You now need to record this transaction in the financial statements.

(m)   What is the entry to record Paula Patel's purchase in Trendy Togs' accounts?

Dr Receivables ledger control account £2,450 Cr Sales £2,100 Cr VAT control £350	
Dr Receivables ledger control account £2,100 Cr Sales £1,750 Cr VAT control £350	
Dr Payables ledger control account £2,100 Cr Sales £1,750 Cr VAT control £350	

(1 mark)

Task 2: 10 marks

You have been asked to help resolve some queries in the financial statements.

You have reviewed the trial balance and have realised that a cash payment of £4,392 for clothes has been entered into the accounts in error as a net amount, rather than a gross amount. This means that the VAT has not been reclaimed on the purchase.

(a) Complete the journal to correct this error. Select the accounts from the following options: Bank; Payables ledger control account; Purchases; Receivables ledger control account; VAT control account.

Dr		
Cr		

(2 marks)

You have been reconciling the Wages control account and have realised that the payroll journal for March 20-6 has yet to be posted to the accounts. You have been given the following information.

	£
Gross pay	3,500.00
PAYE	258.50
Employees' NI	89.40
Employer's NI	92.30

Both employees have opted out of the company pension scheme, so no pension payments are made.

(b) **(i)** What is the journal to post to the March payroll? Select from the correct option.

Dr Wages £3,592.30 Cr Wages control £3,592.30	
Dr Wages £3,592.30 Cr Wages control £3,152.10 Cr HMRC £440.20	
Dr Wages £3,500 Cr Wages control £3,059.80 Cr HMRC £440.20	

(1 mark)

(ii) Indicate the date the payment to HMRC is due for the March 20-6 payroll. Select the correct option.

7 April 20-6	
19 April 20-6	
30 April 20-6	

(1 mark)

Some of the payroll payments Luke has made to HMRC have been late, and he is concerned he may be visited by HMRC. How many years of payroll records must Trendy Togs keep and have available for inspection by HMRC?

(c) Choose the minimum number of years Trendy Togs must keep payroll records available for inspection by HMRC.

1 year	
3 years	
6 years	

(1 mark)

Luke has recently been approached by a clothing supplier that produces clothes in its factories in the Far East. Luke thinks the new lines will increase profits and improve the long-term sustainability of Trendy Togs.

You have investigated the supplier and have found evidence that it pays its workers very low wages. You now believe that you should share this information with Luke.

(d)   Identify the reason you should share your findings with Luke so that Trendy Togs continues to support the principles of sustainability. Select one option.

Luke could use this information to negotiate a lower price from the supplier, which would improve Trendy Togs' long-term profitability further	
Luke may decide that using this supplier will not promote sustainable practices	
Luke may give you a pay rise for highlighting the issue	

(1 mark)

Luke wants to promote sustainability at Trendy Togs. He has identified several actions he could take, but wants to ensure whatever he decides to do is socially sustainable.

(e)   Which one of the following actions will most promote social sustainability? Select the correct option.

Introducing a recycling scheme for old clothes in his shop	
Employing an additional member of staff to help on Saturdays when the shop is busy	
Donating clothing that he cannot sell to a local homeless shelter	

(1 mark)

Luke wants to buy a new till system which will be able to produce detailed information on product sales, as well as managing inventory and producing purchase orders. He wants the information to be available so that the shop staff can make immediate decisions about which items to reorder and which to discount on a day-to-day basis.

(f)   **(i)**   Identify which type of information Luke wants the new till to provide. Select the correct option.

Information at a strategic level	
Information at a managerial level	
Information at an operational level	

(1 mark)

If Luke chooses to implement the new till system, he will have access to big data.

(ii)   Complete the following sentence:

Big data is a large **volume / value** of data that is **easy / difficult** to store using traditional data processing software.

(2 marks)

Task 3: 10 marks

You are reviewing the trial balance and, as part of this process, are reviewing the controls accounts and investigating any items in the suspense account.

You have reconciled the manual payables ledger to the payables ledger control account. Which items below will require adjusting in the payables ledger control account?

(a)   Identify which two items will require an adjustment in the payables ledger control account. Tick the correct options.

A purchase not recorded in the subsidiary account	
Discount allowed debited to the payables ledger control account	
The purchases daybook net total posted to the payables ledger control account	

(2 marks)

You have completed your review of the payables ledger control account and have made the necessary adjustments. The balance on the control account is now £4,109. The total from the cash book payments for March 20-6 of £13,865 has been entered as £13,685. A credit note from a supplier of £450 was accidentally posted to the receivables ledger control account.

(b)   Calculate the correct balance carried down on the payables ledger control account. Tick the correct option.

£3,479	
£3,839	
£4,379	
£4,739	

(1 mark)

Trendy Togs is considering using a computerised accounting system, which would allow it to store documents electronically. Luke has heard there are benefits of storing documents electronically but is not sure what they are.

(c)   Identify two benefits of filing documents electronically. Select two options.

The most recent copy of a document can be easily accessed	
The cost of setting up electronic filing is minimal	
Physical storage space is not required	
The risk of damage due to natural disasters, such as fire or flood, is higher	

(2 marks)

You have reviewed the trial balance, which balances, and have noticed that the balance on the rent payable account looks very low. You investigate this and find that the rent on the shop for the quarter January to March 20-6 of £4,100 was initially posted as a cash receipt and rent received.

(d)   **(i)**   Why did the trial balance not highlight this error?

The debits and credit posted were equal	
The error made the suspense account balance	
The debits and credit posted were not equal	

(1 mark)

You need to post a journal to correct the error in the recording of rent payable.

(ii)   Which of the following entries will correct the error? Select the correct option.

Dr Rent received £4,100, Cr Cash book £4,100	
Dr Cash book £4,100, Cr Rent payable £4,100	
Dr Rent received £4,100, Cr Cash book £4,100	
Dr Rent payable £4,100, Cr Cash book £4,100	
Dr Rent payable £4,100, Cr Cash book £4,100	

(1 mark)

Luke has asked you for a set of draft financial statements to support a bank loan for the business that he is applying for. He has asked you to ensure that 'the final profit is not lower than the draft financial statements'. You are in the process of finishing the period end adjustments and the final profit figure is very likely to be lower.

(e)   Complete the following sentence. Select the correct options.

You **should / should not** give Luke the draft financial statements as the information contained within them is **misleading / materially correct**.

(2 marks)

Neil Clines is a builder who is currently doing some work for Luke at his home. While you are reviewing the trial balance, you identify that shop decoration costs include an invoice for £1,000 dated 31 March 20-6 for decorating a kitchen. You are sure this is a personal expense, rather than a business expense.

(f)   What action should you take? Select the correct option.

Remove the entry from the financial statements immediately	
Discuss the transaction with Luke to find out if it is a genuine error	
Ignore it	

(1 mark)

Practice knowledge assessment 6

Assessment information

Complete all three tasks.

There are 40 marks in the assessment.

Where the date is relevant, it is given in the task data.

Both minus signs and brackets can be used to indicate negative numbers unless the task instructions say otherwise.

Advice

Read each question carefully before you start to answer it.

Attempt all questions. In the exam, the questions will be computer-marked.

You will have 2 hours and 30 minutes to answer all parts of the assessment. This includes 90 minutes for the assessment and a further 60 minutes for reflection and planning as needed.

Task 1: 20 marks

You work for Gupta & Co, a medium-sized firm of accountants run by Suraj Gupta.

You are preparing the financial statements for the year ended 30 June 20-8 for a client, Organic Inkwell Ltd, a small business that produces organic inks. You have been asked to enter some transactions in the accounting records.

(a)   Identify which one of the following transactions will be entered using a journal. Tick the correct option.

The purchase of new equipment with cash obtained via a loan from the bank	
A sale made to a customer on credit	
The gross salaries for June 20-8, along with employer's National Insurance and employer's pension	
Paying the balance on the company credit card by BACS transfer	

(1 mark)

You need to enter a materials purchase into Organic Inkwell Ltd's accounting records. The company has purchased 123 litres of ink base, costing £11.70 per litre, from a supplier on credit.

(b)   **(i)**   Calculate the net cost of the ink base to the nearest penny.

£ [   ]

(1 mark)

(ii)   Identify the journal that will be used to record this materials purchase in the accounting records.

Select from the following options: Inventory; Production; Bank; Trade; Payables ledger control account.

Debit	
Credit	

(2 marks)

Organic Inkwell Ltd makes a specified range of products for its customers. Whenever the inventory level for an ink colour is forecast to go below a defined level, the business produces a set amount of that colour.

(c) What type of costing system would be appropriate for Organic Inkwell Ltd to use? Select the correct option.

Unit costing	
Batch costing	
Job costing	

(1 mark)

On 1 December 20-7 Organic Inkwell Ltd purchased some new equipment costing £4,100, excluding VAT. This equipment is expected to last for four years after which it is expected to have a residual value of £260. The company depreciates equipment from the month of purchase on a pro rata basis.

(d) **(i)** Calculate the depreciation charge on this equipment for the year ended 30 June 20-8.

£ [   ]

(1 mark)

(ii) When you post the depreciation journal, what impact will it have on the statement of financial position? Tick the correct options.

	Increase	Decrease
Assets		
Liabilities		
Equity		

(2 marks)

Organic Inkwell Ltd has completed the year-end inventory count and has asked you to value the following items, to include in the closing inventory valuation.

(e) Calculate the value for each item of inventory in the table below.

	Quantity	Cost per bottle £	Selling price per bottle £	Additional costs to sell per bottle £	Inventory value £
Gold 0.2 litre bottle	5	36.90	60.00	4.50	
Iridescent pink 0.2 litre bottle	2	48.75	72.30	26.55	

(2 marks)

You have now started work on another client, Wittenbury Travel Ltd, and have prepared the payroll for August 20-8.

(f) Complete the table below to show the net pay and the total amount payable to HMRC.

	£
Gross pay	25,480.92
Income tax	1,293.86
Employees' National Insurance	879.61
Employer's National Insurance	1,217.05
Employees' pension contributions	764.43
Employer's pension contributions	1,274.05
Net pay	
Amount due to HMRC	

(2 marks)

On June 20-8, Wittenbury Travel Ltd is holding deposit payments from customers of £76,200.

(g)   Complete the following sentence.

The deposits paid to Wittenbury Travel Ltd by customers will be treated as **prepaid income /
accrued income** in the year-end financial statements.

(1 mark)

Wittenbury Travel Ltd provides travel services to local businesses on credit. Historically, Wittenbury Travel
Ltd's policy for doubtful receivables was to create an allowance for doubtful receivables of 5% of total
receivables at the year end.

This year, Janine Wittenbury, the owner of the company, has asked you to provide only 2%, to keep profits
high. You explain to her that you must apply the accounting principles, and so cannot change the policy
unless there is a valid business reason to do so.

(h)   Which accounting principle is relevant when deciding whether to keep the allowance for doubtful
receivables at last year's level of 5% of receivables?

Tick the correct option.

Prudence	
Going concern	
Consistency	
Accruals	

(1 mark)

Janine Wittenbury wants to significantly increase profits, so is planning to take out a substantial bank loan.
This will fund a large expansion of the business by setting up new shops in new locations. Business profits
have varied significantly over the past few years and the bank has indicated that this may make obtaining
a loan difficult.

Both Janine and the bank are stakeholders in the business and each has their own attitude to risk.

(i)   Identify the attitude to risk of Janine and of the bank. Select the correct options.

	Janine's attitude to risk	The bank's attitude to risk
Risk averse		
Risk neutral		
Risk seeking		

(2 marks)

You have been asked to work on the financial statements of Kessler Ltd, a client that supplies sports equipment to gyms. On one customer's invoice, the net amount for an Ergo rowing machine is £1,249.60. VAT is charged at the standard rate of 20%.

(j)   Calculate the VAT amount.

£ [   ]

(1 mark)

Kessler Ltd raised an invoice for a running machine on 2 August 20-8. The gross amount on the invoice was £2,700 and the customer was offered a prompt payment discount of 2.5% if it paid within seven days. The customer paid on 5 August 20-8.

How much is the VAT on the prompt payment discount?

(k)   Calculate the VAT on the prompt payment discount given by Kessler Ltd.

£ [   ]

(1 mark)

Kessler Ltd rents a warehouse to store inventory of gym equipment, ready to sell. When you review the rent invoices for the year ended 30 November 20-8, you realise the latest rent invoice has not been included.

The last invoice entered into the accounts is for the quarter ended 30 September 20-8.

The annual rent is £18,360, which is invoiced quarterly on 31 March, 30 June, 30 September, and 30 December.

(l)   **(i)**   Calculate the adjustment for the rent to be entered into the November financial statements.

£ [   ]

(1 mark)

(ii)   On which date will the adjustment be reversed in the financial statements?

30 September 20-8	
1 October 20-8	
30 November 20-8	
1 December 20-8	

(1 mark)

Task 2: 10 marks

You have been asked by your manager to help resolve some queries that have been raised by various clients.

Jane Wittenbury, the owner of Wittenbury Travel Ltd, currently processes the payroll and runs the Human Resources function for the business. She is considering outsourcing payroll and Human Resources and has asked about outsourcing.

(a) Identify two positive impacts that outsourcing payroll and Human Resources could have on Wittenbury Travel Ltd. Select two correct options.

Outsourcing payroll is always cheaper than doing the work in-house	
Payroll information may need to be available at an earlier date in the month	
Staff will be available for other work	
The payroll bureau will be responsible for ensuring payroll deductions comply with current legislation	

(2 marks)

Jane Wittenbury is also considering introducing accounting software for her business. She is concerned about how she can keep the data in her business secure and wants to prevent some of the accounts staff from seeing certain sensitive information.

(b) **(i)** How could sensitive accounting information be restricted to authorised individuals? Select the correct option.

Using a firewall	
Using antivirus software	
Using system access levels	

(1 mark)

Jane Wittenbury wants to ensure the data contained in the accounting software system is accurate and complete and wants to know about processing controls.

(ii)   Indicate which of the following controls is a processing control. Select the correct option.

Sequence checking of invoices	
Matching an invoice to a goods received note	
Review and authorisation of a BACS payment to a supplier prior to submission to the bank for payment	

(1 mark)

Jane Wittenbury is keen to ensure she understands the risks that cyber-attacks can pose to the operation of her travel business.

(iii)   Indicate which of the following is a risk a cyberattack poses to the operation of the business. Select the correct option.

Incorrect entry of customer data into the travel reservation system	
Loss of customer data	
Incorrect application of discounts by shop staff	

(1 mark)

Kessler Ltd, a VAT-registered business, has recently received a letter from HMRC informing it of a forthcoming VAT inspection. What is the main reason for HMRC to undertake a VAT visit to a business?

(c)   Identify the main reason HMRC undertakes a VAT visit. Select the correct option.

To identify any VAT fraud that occurs	
To ensure that the business is paying, or reclaiming, the correct amount of VAT	
To increase the amount of VAT collected to meet HMRC targets	

(1 mark)

You are now working on Kessler Ltd's year-end financial statements and have been asked to balance off several general ledger accounts.

(d)   Select two accounts that will not include a balance carried down at the end of the financial year. Tick the two correct options.

Rent payable	
Pensions control account	
Wages account	
Prepaid expenses	

(2 marks)

On 1 December 20-7, the balance on Kessler Ltd's allowance for doubtful receivables account was £5,917. On 30 November 20-8, the balance on the receivables ledger was £103,450. Kessler Ltd expects 4% of these receivables not to pay. The business has not had any irrecoverable debts during the financial year.

(e)   Calculate the balance on the allowances for doubtful receivables: adjustment account at 30 November 20-8 to the nearest £. Indicate if it is debit or credit balance.

£ [   ]   Debit / Credit

(2 marks)

Task 3:10 marks

You assist some clients with producing monthly management reports.

You are reviewing the trial balance for Organic Inkwell Ltd at 31 December 20-8. As part of this process, you are reviewing the controls accounts and investigating any balances on the suspense account.

At the beginning of December, the outstanding balance on the receivables ledger control account was £27,556. During the month, sales made on 30-day credit terms were £33,643. In November, some of the items sold were of poor quality, and so were returned by customers. In December, the business issued credit notes totalling £2,783 for these items. Credit purchases in December were £16,364. Customers all paid during the month in line with credit terms after deducting credit notes issued. There were no other transactions in the month.

(a)   Calculate the balance on the receivables ledger control account at the end of the month to the nearest £.

£

(1 mark)

The non-current assets on the non-current asset register of Organic Inkwell Ltd have been physically inspected and the register has been updated. It has then been compared to the non-current asset: cost account in the general ledger.

The non-current asset: cost account in the general ledger has a balance of £24,189. However, the non-current asset register shows assets with a total cost of £27,978. You have been asked to explain the difference.

(b)   Which two of the following reasons could result in the balance on the non-current asset: cost account in the general ledger being lower than the non-current asset register total? Tick the two correct options.

The accumulated depreciation for the year has been posted to the non-current assets: cost account in error	
The purchase of a new ink mixer for £3,100 has not been recorded in the non-current asset register	
The non-current assets: cost account has not been updated for a stolen computer, costing £600	
The non-current asset register has not been updated for the disposal of an old ink mixer, costing £2,500	

(2 marks)

You have been investigating and correcting errors you have found in Organic Inkwell Ltd's accounts. The suspense account shows a debit balance of £2,187 relating to an unidentified bank payment.

(c)   Identify the entries required to correct the error and clear the suspense account. Tick the correct option.

Debit: Insurance £2,187 Credit: Suspense £2,187	
Debit: Suspense £2,187 Credit: Insurance £2,187	
Credit: Insurance £2,187 Credit: Suspense £2,187	

(1 mark)

You are now reviewing the accounts of Matthews Ltd, a plumbing business.

The balance on the manual receivables ledger control account does not balance with the list of individual account balances in the receivables ledger. You have now identified the following error:

Heavenly Hotel Ltd, a regular customer of Matthews Ltd, paid an invoice for £4,500 for a new bathroom. This payment has been debited to the customer's account in the receivables ledger.

(d)   Complete the following statement. Select the correct options.

To correct this error, you should **debit / credit** the account of Heavenly Hotel Ltd by **£4,500 / £9,000**.

(2 marks)

You are now completing the bank reconciliation for Matthews Ltd at 31 December 20-8. You have compared the cash book and the bank statement and found the following issues. You now need to update the cash book for some of these items.

(e) Which two of the following items need to be updated in the cash book? Select the two correct options.

A customer payment of £1,250 was received into the bank on 31 December 20-8. The remittance was received on 3 January 20-9	
A faster payment of £1,241 dated 3 January 20-9 for electricity used in 20-8 has not been entered into the cash book	
Outstanding lodgements paid into the bank on 29 December 20-8 have not yet cleared the bank	
A bank loan was received directly into the bank on 31 December 20-8	

(2 marks)

John Matthews, the owner of Matthews Ltd, has asked for your help as he finds it difficult to understand financial information. He has heard that accounting software could help him do this. What does accounting software incorporate that could assist in John's understanding of the business?

(f) Identify one feature of accounting software that could help John understand different elements of finance information. Select the correct option.

Automated posting of entries	
A dashboard	
Product codes	

(1 mark)

John has asked you to help him produce a graph that compares this year's sales to last year's sales. Which graph type would be suitable for this?

(g)   Identify the appropriate type of graph. Select the correct option.

A pie chart	
A matrix	
A line chart	

(1 mark)

Practice knowledge assessment 1 answers

Task 1: 20 marks

(a)   Cash sales made to customers in the showroom

(b)   Accrued expense

(c)   Faithful representation

(d)   **(i)**   £1,764 ((£24,000 - £12,240) x 30% x 50%)

        (ii)

Debit	Depreciation charge
Credit	Accumulated depreciation

(e)   £511.60 (£2,558.00 x 20%)

(f)   **(i)**   £42,409.11 (£115,383.33 - £1,696.13 - £72,059.95 + £781.86)

        (ii)   The VAT is due **to** HMRC.

(g)   Net pay: £9,957.35 (£11,375.00 - £621.40 - £455.00 - £341.25)

        Amount due to HMRC: £1,690.60 (£621.40 + £455.00 + £614.20)

(h)   **(i)**   £1,085 (£1,860 x 7/12)

        (ii)   This amount should be recognised as **an asset** in the statement of financial position.

(i)   **(i)**   £9,000 (300 square metres ÷ (100% - 15%)) x £25.50

        (ii)   Fixed cost

(j)   Offer prompt payment discounts to customers

(k)   An example of a liability account would be **customer deposits**.

        The **interest receivable** would be recorded in the financial statements as income.

(l)   The correct entry is to **debit** the cashbook by **£270**.

Task 2: 10 marks

(a)   It provides real time data

(b)   The accounting software will code similar transactions to the same place, saving time

(c)   A dashboard helps users to **highlight key patterns and trends**.

(d)   False

(e)   Data minimisation, purpose limitation, storage limitation, confidentiality

(f)   This adjustment will **decrease output tax** on the VAT Return.

(g)   **(i)**   £930 (£18,600 x 5%)

       (ii)   Credit (because the allowance is being reduced from £1,700 to £930)

(h)   Input tax on entertaining expenses **cannot** be claimed by a business.

(i)   The business **cannot** claim back all the input tax on the computer.

Task 3: 10 marks

(a)   The sales daybook total credited to the receivables ledger control account

A sales returns daybook total posted to the payables ledger account

(b)   Consistency

(c)   Debit: Suspense £1,458

Credit: Rent receivable £1,458

(d)   Unpresented cheques **are not** normally a cash book adjustment.

(e)   You should **credit** the account of Wonderful Wood Ltd by **£7,040**.

(f)   The National Crime Agency

(g)   Tipping off

(h)   False

Practice knowledge assessment 2 answers

Task 1: 20 marks

(a)   Capital and Assets

(b)   Business entity

(c)   £4,000 ((£25,000 - £5,000) ÷ 4)

(d)   £1,300 Cr (£3,200 – (£16,000 - £14,100))

(e)   In its VAT period ended 31 December 20-5

(f)   16 December 20-4 and 21 December 20-5

(g)   During the year the trader must pay **90%** of the estimated annual VAT liability in nine equal instalments.

(h)   **(i)**   £95,400 (6,360 people x £15 per head)

      (ii)

Flexed food sales budget	£98,400*
Sales price variance	£5,248**

*6,560 people x £15 per head

**£103,640 - £98,400

(i)   Irrecoverable debts expense and VAT account

(j)   The financial statements will include an amount of **£640** for **a prepaid expense**.

(k)   Profit will be understated

Non-current assets will be understated

(l)   **(i)**   £61,188 (£111,250 x (100%-45%))

      (ii)   Mark-up percentage would be higher than the gross profit percentage

Task 2: 10 marks

(a)   It will transfer information from the sales and purchases daybooks into the relevant control account automatically

It will automate the period end routine

(b)   Accounting software will automatically balance off and create a brought forward balance for items that are included on the statement of financial position.

(c)   Failure to disclose

(d)   Allowing the needs of future generations to be met without compromising the ability of future generations to meet their own needs

(e)   Pricing jobs to include paying staff a living wage, rather than the legal minimum wage

Ensuring fridges and freezers are replaced with the most energy saving models

(f)   **(i)**   A form showing any benefits in kind an employee has received during the year

(ii)   6 July 20-6

(g)   Transparency, accuracy, and accountability

Task 3: 10 marks

(a)   Items have been despatched to a customer but the inventory records have not been updated

Goods that have been received into inventory were not recorded

(b)   The disposal of two old freezers has not been recorded in the general ledger

A food mixer costing £799 has been stolen

(c)   £10,028 (£6,463 + £3,643 - £78)

(d)   A sundry cash sale received into petty cash but with no petty cash slip created to record it

(e)   (a) and (c)

(f)   To ensure the cash book accurately reflects the bank transactions of the business

(g)   Amy wants to overstate profit in April

Practice
knowledge
assessment 3
answers

Task 1: 20 marks

(a) Going concern

(b) **(i)** £9,500 (£9,200 + £300)

(ii) The purchase of the new digger will **increase** the assets on the statement of financial position.

(c) Accrued expenses

(d) Verifiability

(e) True

(f) Charitable donations

Pension contributions

(g) **(i)** 22 August 20-7

(ii) Three defaults and 1%

(h) **(i)** To assist in planning the timing and value of resources required by Excellence in Recruitment

(ii)

	Budget £	Actual £	Variance £	Adverse / favourable
Labour cost	11,500	12,325	825*	Adverse

*£12,325 - £11,500

(iii) An additional administrator started in September 20-7, which was not planned for

(i)

	£		£
Balance b/d	6,420	Statement of profit or loss	88,760
Cash book	82,340	Balance c/d	0
	88,760		88,760

(j) A bank payment has been allocated to the wrong nominal code

(k) £90 (£650 - £560)

(l) Prepaid income will be shown as **a liability** in the statement of financial position.

Task 2: 10 marks

(a)   The customers of Owen & Sons are **external** stakeholders, whilst the employees are **internal** stakeholders.

(b)   **(i)**   This is an example of **layering**

(ii)   You could be prosecuted for failure to report and fined and/or sent to prison for up to 14 years

(iii)   The Money Laundering Reporting Officer

(iv)   If you have not engaged in money laundering, when you report the money laundering activity, you are making **a protected disclosure.**

(c)   **(i)**   Supplies that are taxed at 0%

(ii)   All of the input tax

(d)   **(i)**   £1,802 ((£79,569 x 5%) - £2,176)

(ii)

Account	
Allowance for doubtful receivables: adjustment	Debit
Allowance for doubtful receivables	Credit

Task 3: 10 marks

(a)   (a) True, (b) False

(b)   Opening inventory plus purchases less closing inventory

(c)   **(i)**

Payment made by Oscar Owen	
Wood and plasterboard costing £3,900 for refurbishing a customer's house	Revenue
A new hammer drill costing £2,300 to replace the previous drill which was purchased several years ago	Capital

   (ii)   Assets and Capital

(d)   **(i)**   Machine data

   (ii)   Veracity: data that is truthful, trustworthy, and accurate

(e)   False

Practice
knowledge
assessment 4
answers

Task 1: 20 marks

(a)   Valuing inventory at the lower of cost and net realisable value

(b)   Decrease the depreciation charge

(c)   **(i)**   Depreciation year ended 31 March 20-3: £17,500.00 x 25% = £4,375.00

Carrying value on 31 March 20-3 = £17,500.00 - £4,375.00 = £13,125.00

Depreciation year ended 31 March 20-4: £13,125.00 x 25% = £3,281.25

(ii)   Carrying value on 31 March 20-4 = £13,125.00 - £3,281.25 = £9,843.75

Depreciation charge year ended 31 March 20-5: £9,843.75 x 25% = £2,460.94

Carrying value when sold = £9,843.75 - £2,460.94 = £7,382.81

Profit/loss on disposal = £5,000.00 - £7,382.81 = £2,382.81 loss

(d)   Hire purchase

(e)   **(i)**   £8,100 ((£15,000 x 20% / 120%) + (£28,000 x 20%))

(ii)   To correct this error, Beautiful Tableware will need to **add this figure to** the **output tax** figure on the current VAT Return.

(f)   **(i)**

Cost card for 600 x 60cm Stoneware circular dish	
	£
Direct materials	1,032*
Direct labour	1,480**
Production overheads	5,470
Total cost of batch	7,982

* 240 kgs x £4.30 per kg

** 600 dishes x 8 / 60 x £18.50

(g)   **(i)**   Prepaid expenses

(ii)

Insurance account			
	£		£
Prepaid expenses reversal	1,690	Prepaid expenses*	1,719*
Bank	6,700	Statement of profit or loss	6,671
Total	8,390	Total	8,390

*£2,292 x 9 / 12

(h)

Account	Debit £	Credit £
Allowance for doubtful receivables: adjustment	3,120.00	
Allowance for doubtful receivables		3,120.00
Allowance for doubtful receivables	514.40	
Allowance for doubtful receivables: adjustment		514.40

Workings:

(£35,460 - £3,120) x 4% = £1,293.60

£1,808 - £1,293.60 = £514.40 required reduction in allowance for doubtful receivables.

Task 2: 10 marks

(a)   Complete and Authoritative

(b)   Column chart

(c)   Visual information can be easier for non-financial managers to understand than tables

The dashboard can be updated to include real-time data

(d)

Statement	True	False
A trial balance produced using a manual system will always balance		✔
A manual system cannot use day books to summarise transactions to post to the general ledger		✔
The receivables ledger control account will automatically agree to the receivables ledger in a manual system		✔

(e)   Motor vehicles

Accrued expenses

Task 3: 10 marks

(a)   **(i)**   £710.94 (£550.30 + £140.65 + £19.99)

(ii)

Element	Increase	Decrease	No change
Assets	✔		
Liabilities		✔*	
Capital	✔		

*As the VAT is recoverable, this will reduce the VAT liability.

(b)   A bank payment made to PL Materials Ltd for £11,987 has been debited in the payables ledger to LP Materials Ltd. This means the trial balance **will** balance.

(c)   The sales daybook, totalling £1,714, was entered into the receivables ledger control account as £1,174

(d)   Bank charges of £63 not yet recorded in the cash book

(e)   Explain to Clare that the inventory value should be correct to comply with accounting regulations

(f)   The supplier's employees are working in safe conditions

(g)   The whereabouts of the laundered property

Practice knowledge assessment 5 answers

Task 1: 20 marks

(a) **(i)** £5,427 (£7,535 - £2,135 + (£85 - £58))

(ii) The balance on the VAT control account will be a **credit**.

(b) £195

(c) 7 April 20-6

(d) Faithful representation

(e) **(i)** £3,580 (£4,200 - £500 - £120)

(ii) The **prepaid expenses** for vehicle costs for the road tax will be reversed on **1 April 20-6**.

(f)

	£
Gross profit *	132,000 (*£220,000 x 60%)
Cost of sales **	88,000 (**£220,000 x 40%)

(g)

	Quantity £	Cost £	Selling price £	Inventory value £
Marble-pattern dress, size 16	2	18.99	39.99	37.98
Lounge trousers, 38" waist 34" leg	3	29.99	19.99	59.97

(h) Budgeting can improve the control and decision making in the business

(i) £385,000

(j) Rolling budget

(k) £42,460 (£17,500 + (£16 x 30 hrs per week x 52 weeks))

(l) **(i)** £1,500

(ii) When an item is not capitalised, the expenses in the statement of profit or loss increase

(iii) The principle of materiality means that the users' view of the financial statements will not change if small items are not capitalised

(m) Dr Receivables ledger control account £2,100

Cr Sales £1,750

Cr VAT control £350

Task 2: 10 marks

(a)

Dr	VAT control account	£732*
Cr	Purchases	£732

*£4,392 x 20/120

(b) **(i)** Dr Wages £3,592.30

Cr Wages control £3,152.10

Cr HMRC £440.20

(ii) 19 April 20-6

(c) 3 years

(d) Luke may decide that using the supplier will not promote sustainable practices

(e) Donating clothing that he cannot sell to a local homeless shelter

(f) **(i)** Information at an operational level

(ii) Big data is a large **volume** of data that is **difficult** to store using traditional data processing software.

Task 3: 10 marks

(a)   Discount allowed debited to the payables ledger control account

The purchases daybook net total posted to the payables ledger control account

(b)   £3,479 (£4,109 + £13,685 - £13,865 - £450)

(c)   The most recent copy of a document can be easily accessed

Physical storage space is not required

(d)   **(i)**   The debits and credits posted were equal

(ii)   Dr Rent received £4,100, Cr Cash book £4,100

Dr Rent payable £4,100, Cr Cash book £4,100

(e)   You **should not** give Luke the draft financial statements as the information contained within them is **misleading**.

(f)   Discuss the transaction with Luke to find out if it is a genuine error

Practice knowledge assessment 6 answers

Task 1: 20 marks

(a) The gross salaries for June 20-8, along with employer's National Insurance and employer's pension

(b) **(i)** £1,439.10 (123 x £11.70)

  (ii)

Debit	Inventory
Credit	Payables ledger control account

(c) Batch costing

(d) **(i)** £560 (£4,100 – £260 x (7 months ÷48 months))

  (ii)

	Increase	Decrease
Assets		✔
Liabilities		
Equity		✔

(e)

	Quantity	Cost per bottle £	Selling price per bottle £	Additional costs to sell per bottle £	Inventory value £
Gold 0.2 litre bottle	5	36.90	60.00	4.50	184.50*
Iridescent pink 0.2 litre bottle	2	48.75	72.30	26.55	91.50**

*5 x £36.90
**2 x (£72.30 - £26.55)

(f) Net pay: £22,543.02 (£25,480.92 - £1,293.86 - £879.61 - £764.43)

  Amount due to HMRC: £3,390.52 (£1,293.86 + £879.61 + £1,217.05)

(g) The deposits paid to Wittenbury Travel Ltd by customers will be treated as **prepaid income** in the year-end financial statements.

(h) Consistency

(i)

	Janine's attitude to risk	The bank's attitude to risk
Rick averse		✔
Risk neutral		
Risk seeking	✔	

(j)   £249.92 (£1,249.60 x 20%)

(k)   £11.25 (£2,700 x 2.5% x 20/120)

(l)   **(i)**   £3,060 (£18,360 ÷ 12 x 2)

      (ii)   1 December 20-8

Task 2: 10 marks

(a)   Staff will be available for other work

The payroll bureau will be responsible for ensuring payroll deductions comply with current legislation

(b)   **(i)**   Using system access levels

(ii)   Matching an invoice to a goods received note

(iii)   Loss of customer data

(c)   To ensure that the business is paying, or reclaiming, the correct amount of VAT

(d)   Rent payable

Wages account

(e)   £1,779 Credit (£5,917 - (£103,450 x 4%))

Task 3: 10 marks

(a) £33,643 (£27,556 + £33,643 - £2,783 - (£27,556 - £2,783))

(b) The accumulated depreciation for the year has been posted to the non-current assets: cost account in error

  The non-current asset register has not been updated for the disposal of an old ink mixer, costing £2,500

(c) Debit: Insurance £2,187

  Credit: Suspense £2,187

(d) To correct this error, you should **credit** the account of Heavenly Hotel Ltd by **£9,000**.

(e) A customer payment of £1,250 was received into the bank on 31 December 20-8. The remittance was received on 3 January 20-9

  A bank loan was received directly into the bank on 31 December 20-8

(f) A dashboard

(g) A line chart